Am I Lost or Was I Never Found?

Shaista Samreen

Dear visitor,
The point of publishing this part of me is to make you feel something. Be it happiness or sadness. I know at some point in your life you might have felt lonely, hurt, hopeless, and many more such emotions that cannot be described in words. I just want you to know that it will get better. It might look like the hurt will never go away, but *it will find a home too, and the home is not you.* It might seem so, but it's just a guest, and it will leave too, like every other guest of yours. I just want you to know that your existence matters so much that if you leave, the darkest clouds will lose the hope to see the light, the rain will lose the hope to see the rainbow, the waves will lose the hope to find their lost drops, the penguins will lose the hope to find their mates, the poetry will lose the will to be written down, and your home will never feel like home again. You alone matter so much. Keeping everything aside, your soul alone is worth something that is not quantitative. Let out the light that you have been hiding inside for so long. Let it out so that you can see it too. For the first time, let your eyes see the truth.

The joy ceased living, and the pain felt so alive.

Rain was pouring like tears from my face; I could barely see the drops, but the clouds were turning empty one by one. I opened the curtains of my room to let some light in, and it did, but it never reached my heart.

I'm not sure what was standing between my heart and this light; *no matter how badly I wanted it to touch my heart, it kept resisting further.*

I stood there with hope, leaving every corner of my heart for the last time.

All I could see was light, but all I could feel was darkness.

"Shai?" mom called.

I wanted to answer, but my shaking voice refused to do so. All I wanted to do was cry until I could cry no more. "Beta, come downstairs; let's have lunch," mom said.

I felt no hunger for food, but only hunger for the will to live.

How do I tell her that I feel like disappearing every now and then?

How can I ever see her beautiful face lose its sparkle because of me?
"I'm coming in 5 minutes," I replied with a heavy heart and deep breaths.

All I needed was 5 minutes to wash my face and appear like I never cried today, so I did and put up a persona, which I normally do, to fool the ones around me into thinking that I'm living a life far from blue.

– 5 minutes

"there are people who have it worse"
I wish these words could take away my suffering
and wash my trauma away like rain.

I know they have a broken limb, and all I have is a
strain, and I'm at a loss for what to do.

Pain is difficult to quantify; when something hurts,
it hurts.
It doesn't matter if it's a cut or a wound.

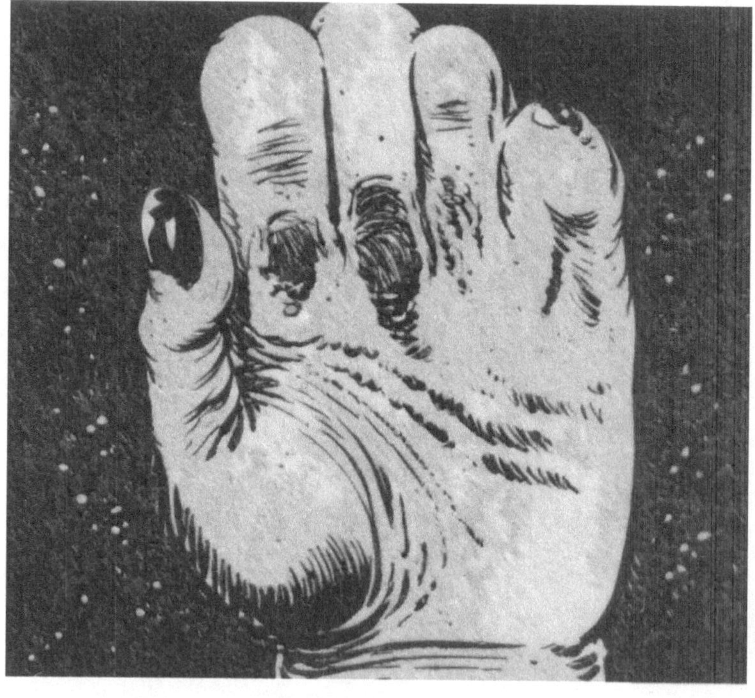

Stages:

Stage one

When you don't know what's going on!

Stage two

When you realise that your whole life you have
been fooled

Stage three

When you finally feel your soul bleed

Stage four
When you spend counting days leading so sore

Stage five
When you don't want to die but want to give up on
life,
Stage six

When you can't find the fix,

Stage seven

when you go on the internet until 4:11

Stage eight

When you start cursing your fate,

Stage nine

When nothing satisfies you, with your life, nothing
rhymes.

Stage ten

You feel nothing, your soul dies.

Tsunami of feelings:

The human heart is susceptible to heartbreak.

Yet the tsunami of feelings finds a home inside.

The bitter pain comes in waves and lingers in
the shallow void.

It shall pass with time.

But will time fix the scars it will leave behind?

Or will I learn to live in affliction?

Will I learn to watch my feelings collide?

Happy kid:

A little dusky girl

With butterflies on her shirt

Smiling through the day

Making cookies out of clay

pink bow on her hair, heading to the fun

fair, twirling in her dress,

going crazy with childishness.

She's the happy kid.

But she's going through some things

She's a happy kid, but she's swallowing up

her fears.

She's the happy kid.

The tag doesn't seem to fit.

She's the happy kid.

Is she really it?

It's almost bedtime.

She's changing into her pyjamas.

A pastel pink one with some blueish flares

Singing herself some sad lullabies

People are always engaged in their bitter lies.

She's a happy kid, but she's going through some things.

She's a happy kid, but she's dying because of her fears.

She's the happy kid, but the tag doesn't seem to fit.

She's the happy kid.

Is she really it?

Now this happy kid isn't happy anymore.

This happy kid wants some friends to play along.

But the castle's guards won't let anyone in.

This happy kid wants to run away, but she's been
watched by everyone.

Oh, she's not a happy kid.

She's going through a lot of things.

She's not a happy kid; she's grounded by her fears.

She's not a happy kid; the tag doesn't fit; it's

obvious.

She's not a happy kid.

Is she really it?

She was never it.

– Happy kid

Past life:

It rained last day,

When I was on my way

My feet hit a puddle of water.

I saw a reflection, and I lost her.

I kept on walking and walking.

I realised I had lost my sense of belonging.

I suddenly stopped at an old house.

It was broken, and I heard someone shout

I went inside to keep a check

It was so cold, it almost froze my bones.

"So you are back," a voice murmured.

I got chills down my spine as soon as I heard her.

I looked for the closest escape but could see

none.

I closed my eyes and tried to run.

Something hit my legs, and I fell so hard.

That was the day when I lost myself.

We are running out of time.

Posting pictures of yourself smiling Does

that mean you're happy, or are you just

pretending?

I am scared that we might lose her now. I

found a letter in her closet.

Now I can't speak.

My voice is gone.

I found a letter in her closet.

I don't want to read it.

I am dumb.

I don't want to let you go.

I wish you could just come back for once.

I wish I could be there for you.

I wish I was good enough.

I want to say something.

But I know you wouldn't listen.

Now you are gone.

- letter to self

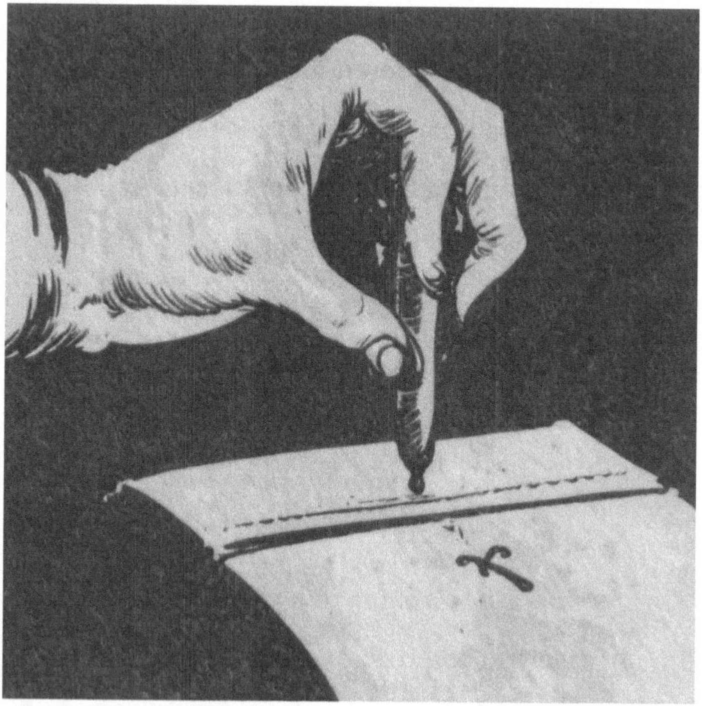

I wish i could hug my younger self:

I was running down the streets of my broken
self-esteem.
Everything I did seemed to offend somebody.
Every time I shouted, I would hit my
head on the wall.
The blood would leave the stains, and I would
cover them all.

Every thing I tried didn't give my heart the
rest. But when your soul is tired, nothing
could can be said.

I isolated myself from every mess. But now I
feel I have lost emotional sense.

I wish I could hug my younger self.
Because she was hurt.

A blind man can still see things. It takes
more than vision to see things; it takes
the capacity to see beyond the realm of
the physical world.

What if i dissappeared?:

Nowadays, nobody notices

The pain hidden behind your smile

I have tried talking to people about it.

But they didn't feel like they really cared enough

to help.

Oh, every day I cry myself to sleep.

Under the blanket, so my parents won't hear my

weeping.

Oh, every day I feel like I am lost.

I'm trying to find myself, but I don't know how.

Sometimes I wonder what will happen.

If one day I disappeared just like the dragons

Would people care or wouldn't?

Would they even know that I am not here

anymore?

Would they even shed a tear for me?

Or they would post sad things on the internet

while smiling.

Nowadays, everything feels

against me.

I keep on laughing while I

bite my tongue under my

teeth.

I have tried so hard to let it

go.

But some things break you

harder.

Your soul is harder than your

bones.

Oh, every day I cry myself to sleep.

Under the blanket, so my parents won't hear my weeping.

Oh, every day I feel like I am lost.

I'm trying to find myself, but I don't know how.

Sometimes I wonder what will happen.

If one day I disappeared just like the dragon

Would people care or wouldn't?

Would they even know that I am not there anymore?

Would they even shed a tear for me?

Or they would post sad things on the internet
while smiling.

Sometimes I feel like this world is too busy for doing nothing. People are roaming here and there but end up nowhere. Then I ask myself, Is it important to end up somewhere? Or can I just roam here and there like a lost star? But even stars have a home to go to; they mix with the sand and find a hand to hold. not in a literal sense; I mean a hand to hold, but a wind that makes me feel like I am at home. How does it feel to be at home? Is it an imaginary feeling that people invented to not feel alone, or am I cursed to not be able to know? Is it when I lay my head down on my mom's lap and get lost in her beautiful scent? Or is it when I hug my father and feel safe and loved? Can I have different homes, or is it just a perfect one? Are there still perfect things? or is it just a word left in the dictionary? Is it when I write down my feelings on a piece of paper? Am I building my home to build me up? Am I so fragile to rely on a piece of paper for my home?

or are the words that I pen down, and with every word, I feel closer to home? What if there was nothing as paper and nothing as writing known? How would I let this weird feeling out of every single bone? I ask too many questions, I know, but isn't that the point of existence? How can I live without knowing the secrets of living? Am I living yet or not? Am I still unlocking the doors that would lead me to the treasure of the secrets of living? or am I losing the key to it even though the treasure is right in front of me? I question this every single day: What's the point of living? not because I am hopeless or disappointed, but just out of curiosity, I ask this question. There is no crime in it, I suppose. Even if it's a crime, I am not scared to be a criminal. Everyone is a criminal in one way or another; some kill others, while others kill themselves without a funeral.

Am I alive? Have I yet committed the crime? I won't kill anyone, *but am I safe for myself?*

These questions keep haunting me every now and then.

Maybe someday I will find the key to the treasure that will reveal all the secrets. If I have the key with me, I might be a treasure indeed.

– Home

I see people as not just people anymore but as souls who are longing to be known, not by people but by themselves. Who is she? Who is he? Who are they? We tend to ask these questions, but do we ever wonder who we are? We are so willing to know people that we forget that we don't come up with our own system manuals; we need to write them for us. Am I calling us machines? no. but I think we are like machines in a way. The only difference is that you and I break down into oceans of tears sometimes, and it can't be fixed with a new battery or oil. We crave time to heal ourselves, but time is not the saviour. It's us who accept that nothing can be completely fixed once broken; like how a broken machine misses the old parts of its own, we miss them too. But man, oh man, I wish we could replace them that easily like how machines do, but we have something as memory, but memories fade away too.

But why do I still feel like a part of me is gone somewhere on a little trip?

I don't know if it's a round trip or a one-way trip.
If it's a round trip, I'll meet it again, but if it's a
one-way trip, I'll miss it every moment.

– Trip

It's all red. I see everything in the palette of red. Sometimes it's too deep, and sometimes it's lighter, but it's always red. I look like the shades of blue they say; I think I'm purple from inside. The blue mixes so well with the red, leaving the purple in its wake. But nobody knows that I'm purple. If they got to know, would they care to stay? Would they try to get rid of the red so that it doesn't turn purple? or would they lie to me and say I'm not purple?

Do they only like me when I'm blue and not purple?
Would they try to paint me blue if I turned into a different colour? What if they already did? and I am unknown to this fact.
People are so busy painting other people all the time that they forget their own colour.
They forget if they were once blue, purple, or red. They get confused and see themselves in the shades of white and black. White, I say is easier to be painted again, but black hides everything that goes into it. Those who consider them white are less likely to be it.

They hide shades of malice and anger in them.
Those who are black are less likely to be it; they
hide shades of love and comfort in them. I'm not
being racist about the colours; colour is never an
issue; it's the words that can even make a rose
sound like a shroud.

– purple

People say I am like sunshine; I shine, and they say it's very bright. I see myself as a dark void where my own light cannot reach. How cursed can one be? People keep telling me that I am a star and that I was born to shine.

But in a universe full of stars, I think I am a meteor. As I am falling, I am shining. They can see the light because it's so bright, but I only see myself falling into the void. Am I blind to my own light? Does that make me a blind person after all? But if I can see the light that others shine, why can't I see my own light? Is the intensity too high for my eyes? or is it because I am blind? My heart sees better visions of the things that scare me the most, but not my own light. Will I ever see it in this lifetime? Will I ever be mine?

My soul craves you, but my body aches for you.

You are bad for me, but my mind can't digest

this truth.

I can't afford to live in a universe without you.

but it keeps hurting me as I get closer to you.

It's not the same for *you;* you are loved

and adored.

I'm just a part, and for me, you were my whole

Let me go for once, and I will never return to

you.

Let me suffer before I come back to you.

Let me take a sip before I turn into ashes and

bones.

– to the girl in the mirror

Sometimes I sit under the sun and let the light cover the darkness inside of me. With this hope, I search for the sun every day. People say it comes out every day, but does it come to everyone every day? I don't think so. If it comes out every day for everyone, then how come some can only see the darkness? or is it because their eyes are covered with the web of their thoughts? or is it just the sun? Is it because their hearts are beating at a slower pace? or is it just the sun? Is it because their brains are crumbling with the broken shreds of their dreams? or is it just the sun? Is it because they have lost some parts of themselves that they never wanted to? or is it just the sun? Is it because they have turned out to be someone else? or is it just the sun? What is the sun?

Is it just a blazing hot ball, or can it be anything that gives warmth to your soul? Is it when I meet the people I love the most, or is it when I see myself happy in the mirror?

Is it when someone calls me kind, or is it when I
eat ice cream and a few drops melt on my hand?
What is the sun?

Why does it hide sometimes?

– The sun

I no longer believe in love, for god's sake.

My shadow left me too, in the dark.

How can I ever find it again?

When I'm blind to its mark

"Hello, are you there "? I scream

Am I deaf, or is this all a dream?

I feel so separate from myself.

I'm the book no one ever bothered to read.

Will someone ever read my story?

Will I ever witness this glory?

"I'm here," but you never stayed to listen.

You ran away in a few seconds.
If this is what they call love?

A bullet disguised as a rose

With only thorns and no beauty at all

How can you blame the shadow?

When were you the one to leave first?

The farthest ray of light touched your skin.

You left me here and ran away to follow it.

I tried to read your story, and I surely did.

I found no verse of mine; you forbid.

You never wanted to be read by me,

because when I did,

you lost the sense to see

How can you blame the shadow?

I never left; you turned blind to me.

You wanted the light, and I wanted you to find me.

You wanted the love, and I felt the pain.

How can you ever blame the shadow, silly?

You were too busy learning to swim in the sea. You
forgot there's beauty in drowning; that's when you
forgot about me.

-Thee shadow

We were never friends nor enemies; we just didn't exist for each other.

We would part ways when told to stay together. We would just ignore each other. But time can make a lot of changes.

You became my buddy, and I became your friend. We would laugh at the stupid jokes we made, and we would cry together on our bad days.

But as it wasn't meant to be forever, you parted ways again.

You left me feeling like you were never here. Now I think maybe that wasn't even that important to you,

but then I remember you texting me "hey" whenever you felt the blues.

Now I am left with all the bittersweet memories. I think one day you will come and say to me, I am sorry for hurting you.

I want to be your friend one more time, my lost friend.

And I would reply, "*You mean to be friends and then strangers again?*"

- I lost a friend

I met you when you were going through your
darkest phase.

You told me I was like an angel sent from heaven
above.

I took a part of myself and filled your empty space.
Just so you could leave me like you were never here
False assurances

I know how it is.

I know that you don't care about me.

That's why you seem so happy.

Without me in your life,

It's a truth that I wish I could deny.

Despite everything that I have done for you, You
treated me like a fool.

I tied your shoelaces. So you won't fall down.
But then I stepped on mine. And you weren't there
to help me out.

Without a doubt

I never fit into these crowds.

– Tied your shoe laces

I want to run away from reality.
But it runs faster than me.

I want to run away from people.

But they want my company.

— reality

Ever wondered?:

Ever wondered why we lie?

Ever wondered why we hate goodbyes?

Ever wondered why we see things that aren't
real?

Ever wondered why we cut lines and then conceal
them?

Ever wondered why we hate?
Do you want to be the culprit?

Ever wondered why we love?

Do you don't want your heart to be broken?

Ever wondered why we are here?

Ever wondered why we fear?

Ever wondered why we envy?

Ever wondered why we are so greedy?

Ever wondered why we don't learn the lesson

at once?

Ever wondered why we regret after doing a

crime?

Ever wondered why we give?

Do we get back to what we were thinking?

Ever wondered why we plead?

We ourselves are so damn sensitive.

Ever wondered why we leave?

Ever wondered why we disbelieve?

I told myself

It's alright if they don't really want you.
I told myself all the things I wanted someone else
to tell me too.

Ever wondered why we cry?
Ever wondered why we smile?
Ever wondered why we dream?
Ever wondered why things end?

Tell me why you have to be so worried about how
I perceive?

Tell me how it matters if I am fat or if I am
skinny?

Tell me why you have to be so mean, young men
and ladies.
Tell me, why can't you be you, and why can't you
just let me be me?

God is the one:
sleepless nights, yeah, I am sleep deprived.
rocket science, yeah, I am rocket science.

Nobody gets me these days.

Empty promises,

taking away my good girl faith

Something's wrong in the air.
Every time I go on a rollercoaster, I come out to
be even stronger.

I have the best company in the world.

God is the one, yeah. I don't feel incomplete.

Till God is with me

I don't let the shade get to me.

Till God is with me
Because God is the one.

Empty hearts, yeah, I love empty hearts.

Good things fall apart, but bad things never last.

I don't need anyone to get me

These pretty pink skies,

Giving me positive energy

I have longed for it all my life.
Every time I go on a rollercoaster, I come out to
be even stronger.

I have the best company in the world.

God is the one, yeah. I don't feel incomplete.

Till God is with me

I don't let the shade get to me.

Till God is with me
Because God is the one.

Paper town:

It's the same town.

But is it the same now?

The same scenery but a different crowd.

The sky is weeping.

The people are grieving.

This paper town is so deceiving.

The houses are turning wet.

With the shower of the sins

The people are showing their colours,
Under the silhouettes
They are feeling ashamed,
For misleading their palletes
This paper town is to blame.
The paper town is stained.

Tranquility:
The tantalising scent of the old books
The fond memories of childhood
The serenity of the stars
The coffee in jars
Is nothing but the illustration of tranquilly for
me.

The calmness of the silence
The freedom of the sky
The sound of the waves
The solace in sighs
Is nothing but the illustration of tranquilly for
me.
The warm hugs of mother
The sweet heeds of father
The pure love of a brother
It smothers your life in colour.
It's nothing but the illustration of tranquilly For
me.

The good days after the bad ones
The group calls with whimsical friends.
The iced slushie needs no amends.
The dark days are blending into bright ones.
Is nothing but the illustration of tranquilly for
me.

When the sky gets dark and the weather is gloomy, you come out as the sun and show people something that is the most expensive form of anything: *hope*. You appear like that one star that shines in the night sky, and people see you and pray to God through you.

You are like the prettiest rose, but the thorns get you every time. But every beautiful thing must be hard to get, right? It's the thorns that make you even more beautiful. You are like the end of a tunnel one sees at the end of darkness, and you are the light that peeks through it. You might ask, Why are you the light? To be honest, I don't know exactly why, but some people are just so bright that there is no need to find a reason. Maybe there is no reason for this brightness, or maybe there is, but the point is that you are the light in both ways.

By light, I don't mean a beam of rays; by light, *I mean a reason to hold onto, a reason to be hopeful, a reason to live, and a reason to smile.*

Maybe your darkness inside is eating you up inside, but in the end, the light always wins. Nothing can be stronger than that. Let your soul guide you to the light of your own, and you shall see it too one day, and that day you will know why you are the light. Maybe you can see it in little things, like when somebody's face lights up when they see you or when you do something that makes people smile. It's always the ones who radiate the energy, like you. You share your light with others, and it reflects back to you. You might assume it's them, but it's you. You can see your own light in others.

— you are the light

Sunny days:
Sunny days are coming.
to melt my stone-cold heart

Lightning strikes the ground.

My soul gets an electric shock.

That day when I lost myself

My pillow couldn't handle it.

I cried too many times.
I thought I would stay by my side.
yet I feel sunny days are coming.
To bring the light into my life
Maybe I lost myself to find a new me.
Maybe it's about the perception and not the tragedy.

So no one told you, kid.

Life was going to be this way.

Paper towns, paper people

Burning thoughts turned to ashes.

Losing friends, losing temper

Losing everything I have ever had

I don't want to lose myself.
But it feels like there's no escape.

I don't know when I will feel okay.

I feel like I am grounded by a thousand serpentines.

If only I knew how and what to say.

I wouldn't be so lost in my

messed-up head.

The clouds are moving on, so why don't we?
Let the past be in the past and set ourselves
free.

Phases of the moon:
Like phases of the moon I shine, and I hide.

I live and I die.

I fear, and I fight.

I crawl, and I walk tall.

I lose, and I win. I fall, and I rise.

Like phases of the moon

I learn, and I teach. I love and I preach.

I hate it, and I flinch. I cry, and I grinch.

Like phases of the moon
A part of me is always lost.

And when I find that part of mine,

That's when they call it a full moon.

That's when they call it intune.

That's when they call it a pleasant perfume.

That's when they call it a perfect afternoon.

That's when they call it a summer night in June.

"I am there for you."

But then why do I feel so alone even
in a crowded room?

I am happy:

These days, even the darkness seems alright to me.

The waves seem to make a painting of mine in the
sea.

Even the clouds are moving on, so why don't we?

Let's leave the past in the past and set ourselves
free.

I am happy.

I feel so free to be me.

I might not make a lot of friends.
But the ones I keep are my true gems.

I was once lost and loud.

But now, when I look back, I just laugh around
like it was fun.

I might have left some people behind.

But they better know the reason themselves.

Some days I teleport to my imaginary land.

To get away from all the pain I have had in the

past.

People started to leave, like they were never here.

Left me with the belief that their trust is forever
dead.

But now I am happy.

I love me, and that's not easy.

I let them go:

People become my friends for a period of time. I
was okay without them, and now I am not fine.

They keep showing how they are crying outside.

I wonder if they know that I am dying inside.
Even after giving it a thousand tries, I couldn't hold
it all inside.

after burning myself a million times.

Finally, my ashes cry.

So I let them go.

I heard that they made some new friends.

Meanwhile, I am here, trying to figure myself out.

Everything that has happened is messing with my
head.

They are there hanging out while I am stuck in bed.

Even after giving it a thousand tries, I couldn't hold
it all inside.

After burning myself a million times,
Finally, my ashes cry.

So I let them go.

One day, I wish

They find a friend just like them.

Then they will realise that

How cruel of them to make me question my
existence!

I still feel their absence.

I am losing my mind's balance.

But still, I let them go.

At the end, it doesn't even matter.

I let them go.

At the end, it won't even hurt that bad.

I let them go.

At the end, it will heal the wounds better.

I let them go.

Some days feel like they will never end.

We try to blame ourselves and search for
amends.

the weight of a bullet running through your
brain.

Is it similar to yelling, "I hate who I am?"

When you are ready to give it all up, Hold on for
a moment.

The end is not bitter.

When you are so low, you act so high. Remember
all the times you fought for their lies?

People only care when you leave them behind.

Don't lose yourself in this fight.

Hold on for a second.
The end is way better.

In the end, it's you and your past.

Not all stories end up like the rest.

And when you try to open up,

They shut you up to save themselves.

Hold on for now.

The end is good somehow.

After it's all said and done

The regret of not standing up for yourself eats
you up.

Nobody is going to search for what you have lost.

Push them away and go back to where you belong.

Hold on you are strong.

– hold on

Flower garden:

There are so many flowers around.

Different scents and different colours

Why would anyone ever pick me?

I am not like the others.

The bees go to the ones who look attractive.

The bees suck their sweetness and leave them all
distracted.

Why would they ever pick me?

I am radioactive.

I never imagined being chosen.

But imagination is not always real.

Some angels came and watered me.

My heart cried, and my eyes concealed

In this huge flower garden,

Why did you choose the most different one?

I asked

"In this huge flower garden.

We chose the most reclusive one."

The angels replied.

Fall before rise:

Birds fall and try

Birds fly and rise.

That's the reason why

They excel in the alluring sky.

Reality doesn't always cross

The path to our wants

It makes us feel lost.

Like warmth in the frost

When it's all said and done,

We hide from the present and try to run.

Away from reality, as it is brutal truth
Our hearts' filled with regret and Ruth

Why do we lose hope after we fall?

Falling makes us rise even taller.

So let's not agonise about the writings on the
wall.

It's about how we respond to stumbling blocks,
after all.

If ever you feel like quitting,
Remember why you even started?
The plane has already departed.

With your dreams and desires together, bonded.

Raindrops taught me the biggest lesson.

They fall from the sky and rise up to heaven.

Nothing can compare to their obsession. About

falling first and rising higher than Revon

Pack your bags and get ready.
The hurdles are never-ending.

Let your power be mightier than the problem.

Be ready to fall and rise again until you

overcome.

Some days are harder than others.

But golden days come after the bad ones.
We just need to accept the fact that it's human.

To not be okay all the time

Little soldier, I know you will rise.

Rise like the day

Rise unafraid

Rise and shine.

Until falling, don't scare you at any time.

Crowded:

I walk these crowded streets, and the times are
getting so long.

I have spent my whole life thinking,

Where do I really belong?

Maybe it's better for me to learn the lessons twice.

I don't ever learn them on the first try.

No one is with me; I walk alone.

In this world, I have created on my own.

Boys can cry too:

As a kid, I was good at hide and seek.

Even now, I'm hiding something that's making
me weak.

And i am so unclear.

And I am swallowing my fears.

Now that I am older, I feel things way too deeply.

Everything I do seems to offend somebody.

But everyone tells me you can't shed a tear.

So stumbling blocks and heavy rocks are all
meant for me?

But I am going to ball my eyes out
Boys can cry too out loud.

Because I do, and I want you too.

Don't hide behind the blues.

If boys can laugh

Then boys can cry too.

Everyone tells me I look less of a boy.

I don't look like those stalwart guys.

And now, I feel so lost.

And I am keeping my tears inside.

Now that I am older, I can see everything I do
seems to offend somebody

But everyone tells me you can't shed a tear.

So stumbling blocks and heavy rocks are all meant
for me?

But I am going to ball my eyes out

Boys can cry too out loud.

Because I do, and I want you too.

Don't hide behind your blues.

If boys can smile

Then boys can cry too.

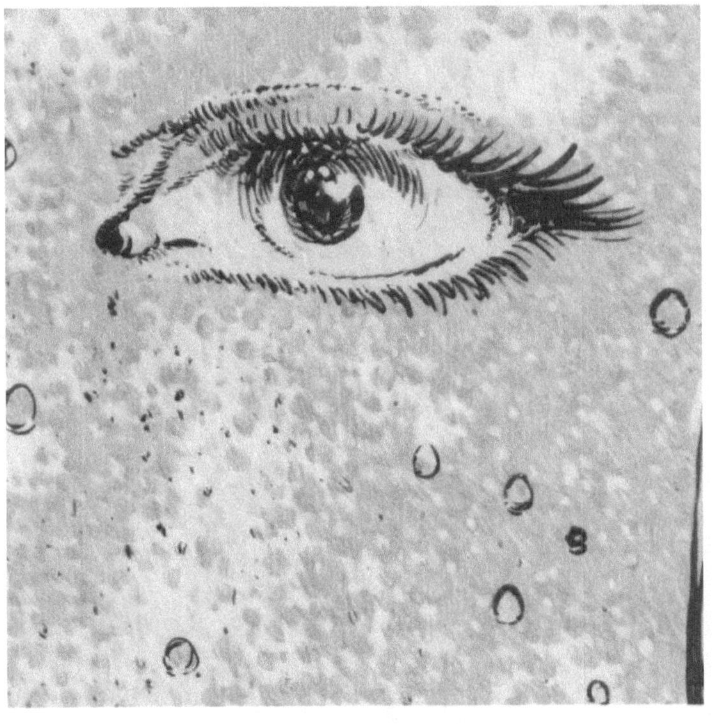

Tears fall sans questioning for gender.
who are we to rule them?

Summer nights in the dark

I try to find the stars that I have lost.

I'm moving on with the waves.

They hit the rocks.

And I am all lost again.

Nobody understands why you are a certain way.

They don't seem to care at all.

I know I am a little weird.

This life seems like a crazy ride.
Am I lost, or was I never found?
Everyone I know is doing great.
Feels like their lives are sorted out.

Am I lost, or was I never found?

I know I am a little weird.

But that's okay, because I am who I am.

It doesn't matter if I am lost or found.

Everyone I know is doing great.

Or maybe they are lost, like I am.

It doesn't matter if we are lost or found.

Am i getting stronger?

I have been keeping things to myself.

I don't trust anybody at all.

People act like they are your friends.

When the truth is something else,

As I grew up, I learned to be stronger than before.

I might not win the battle, but I will surely win the war.

And every time I let them in, They watched me get burned.

And if they think I am still the same,

Then I'm sorry. Better go home.

Healing hurts:
I remember when I was young.

I used to play with my soft toys because I had no
friend to spend time with

They were all different.

Maybe I was indifferent

But I don't think so.

I need to let go of somethings

I know it's hard sometimes to even fake a smile.

but when you have a heart of gold

You pretend you're fine.

for your loved ones.

all the storms you faced alone,

in your own company.

I know that healing hurts.

but this pain is worth it.

You will be fine.

You will be alright.

A girl who knew everybody:

head in the clouds your feet on the ground

Tell me how it feels.

to be you
because you are so cool
You are living my dream.

Let me say

every time I felt like an outcast.

I put the blame on myself.

as if I were made from a different mould?

Oh my god

The screaming, the crying, the fighting,

the urge to find out who I was

in a room full of people who made me feel like a
lost cause

I don't care what you think about me.

I am just here, living my dream.

I know how it feels to be nothing but something.

My Condolences:

My condolences to the people who lost me

I cried oceans of tears.

But now I will shed a tear with them.

As they lost me, I found me.

I send my condolences to them with a heavy heart.

My heart is not heavy for me.

But for them, as they no longer have me.

Monsters:

I remember when I was a child.

I was so scared of the dark.

I thought the monsters would creep inside my bed,
and then I would lose my mind.

As I grew up, I learned to be just fine.

With the darkness inside of me

The world turned out to be a different place. With
monsters disguised as human beings

I told myself It's fine, darling.

Whatever you choose, Just make sure You never
let in

Anyone who ever fooled you

These monsters

They hunt for them.

Who is too good to be true?

So I told myself
Never turn into these cold monsters
Because it's not you.

I need a moment to say it out loud.

The monsters I am talking about

They look completely fine.

Until you let them into your life

They wreck every part of you.

The ones you once used to love

Now you are left with nothing but an unlocked
fear of those parts .

I told myself It's fine, darling.
Whatever you choose, Just make sure You never
let in

Anyone who ever fooled you

These monsters

They hunt for them.

Who is too good to be true?
So I told myself
Never turn into tese cold monsters
Because it's not you.

Unsaid words:

Unsaid words Some words are better left unsaid.
They either give you hope or leave you hopeless.

In the choices of this world, we often tangle
ourselves.

With our priorities like a spider's web

Lost friends and old trends can never be the same.

Reality hits harder when you are on the edge of
living life in pain.

Some stories are better left incomplete.

They either give you peace or leave you in pieces.

You are supposed to be completely fine when you
are in your 20s.

My mom still feels lost sometimes, and she is in her
40s.

My dad still cuts his finger with the knife, and he is
in his 50s.

Age can't decide anything;
it's all about the lessons. S
Some people can tell you the most about life at the age of

11.

Some secrets are better left as secrets.

They give you butterflies or leave you with
goosebumps.

And when it's all said and done,

We get those adrenaline rushes, and our feelings
run

It's finally the day we never wanted to come.

"Goodbye to the ones who will miss me;
I will miss them too."
Something made me feel like my time has come.
So the last goodbye is most likely to be
unsaid.

Unsaid. Yeah, some words are better left unsaid.

They remind you about the good times and the bad
times in an instance.

Oh, these days, I can't sleep.

They say I am pretending.

Take me to the therapist.

You are fine. That's what they say.

I never thought that this earth was such a wild

place.

People here keep gossiping about strangers.

They say, "Let's move to the moon."

"Why not make the earth worth living on"?

I seriously don't have a clue.
What am I even doing here?
What am I even doing here?

They always keep an eye on you,

to point out your mistakes.

It doesn't matter if you are nice.

For them, that is not the case.

made me sad about myself.

then ask, "Why do I act like this?

"Calling people ugly does not make you any

prettier".

body-shaming people

Oh, what a shame on you.

Then they say, "Don't exaggerate your own issues."

They say, "Let's move to the moon.
"Why not make the earth worth living on?
I seriously don't have a clue.
What am I even doing here?

Would it make any difference?
If the same people went to a different place.
They say, "Let's move to the moon.
"Why not make the earth worth living on?

Why is the pain crawling into my veins?

making it hard for me to stand on my knees,
making me so weak.

I might fall any second.

I have lost track of reality.

But I feel the pain so deeply.

Yet I ask again.

Where is my anesthesia?

You are like the waves of the ocean.

So calm, like a tranquil potion

You are like the sound of bugs on a summer evenmg.

You give the soft breeze a deep meaning.

You are like what they call "silence is bliss.

You are like what they call an enchanted abyss.
You are like what they say: "fairytales exist."
You are like someone's deep-prayed wish.

Can you hear the screams in my silence?

Why don't we hear the pain, just the sirens?

Can you feel the hurt in my silence?
Why don't we feel the numbness before the
absence?

Can you see the dullness in my silence?

Why don't we see the signs before it's too late?

Can you let me stay in my loud silence?
loud enough to make me lose my mind.

Is it winter already? I got frostbite.

The sun is shining bright, yet I feel so cold.

The people are enjoying themselves together, but I
want to stay alone.

They are feeling the light, but I am the one stuck
in the black hole.

Is it winter already?

My soul feels so cold.

My limbs are frozen, and my heart is numb.

My brain is working, and my thoughts are
scrambling.

My body is shivering, and my voices are screaming
"overcome."

Is it winter already? I got frostbite.

The coldness inside me is enough to frostbite me.

Paper people:

I lost another buddy of mine.

Not to an accident or death, but to the tragedy of our destiny.

I will keep the Polaroids in my memory box.

Wherever you go, I hope you miss us.

The sound of your laughter, the sound of your acoustic guitar, It is like a sweet old song in my favourite playlist,

I don't know why it happened.

I don't know the motive behind it.

I know that you will forever be my best friend.

Even if you make a new one,

I hope you can regain the peace you lost in me.

I wish I could erase my name from your mind
forever to make it better for you,

If I ever made you laugh, don't forget it.
I pour from my empty cup just for the people I love.

I hope you sometimes feel your heartbeat and think

of me.

Because when it's me, I think of you

Maybe someday I will be the friend you need.

A day with no regrets and no complaints
A day with good memories to make

I will look forward to a day like that.

Till then, goodbye, my buddy.

To the buddy whom I lost or maybe never had.

People change:
Isn't it funny how people change?

Like honey in different seasons

When it's cold outside, they stay.

When it's summertime, they run away.
My inner self warned me to be careful with
whom I trust.

But I still give my all to

The people who didn't even have my back

Laying in my bed

Feeling all broken

Craving to cry

My mind is all frozen.

I just want to know why it's always me, though.

They are fighting.

I am feeling so anxious.

Chills in my spine

I want somebody to stop it.

But nobody's around.

It's just me and my lost self.

I just want to know why it's always me, though. My
grades are getting worse.

How can I concentrate?

With a mind that isn't whole
I just feel like a broken circuit.

Am I even worthy of living this life?

I just want to know why it is always me.

Oh, one day, I will go.

To a world where I will be loved

One day, I will go.

To the world where I won't be judged

One day, I will go.

To the world, I hope you won't be there too. One
day, I will go.

To a place where I can love myself

But I won't go on my own.

God knows when it's my time to go.

My body is so hard that I can't even move a thing.

Thin or fat, it really defines who I am.

Oh, what a shame. Oh, what a shame.

I have been talking to myself.
No one speaks my language.

I tried to make it clear.

But still, they said it was blurry as hell.

Guess what happens when you don't want to care?

Black and white It's all I listen to.

But one day, I will go.

I'm sorry if I offended you with my poem.

I know I don't belong.

But it's all I know going on.

So do something for it, or just stay numb.

Your wings broke, and you can't fly anymore.
But your vision is fine; you can make these broken
wings work.

Are you feeling a little low, or is that not the issue?

Or is it the feeling of letting go of your sorrows?

When you enter the dark, does your shadow get rid
of you?

Or maybe your shadow is always with you, but you
want to let it go.

When you are tired of all this, you want to let
yourself go.

To a place where nobody knows your name, so you
can start a little bold.

But, my dear, it's not a Mario game.

Where in you die and revive again.

It's a beautiful ballad, with all the scenes
intermixed.

Live it and smile too.

But don't die before your death, you fool.

Healing is like medicine,
tastes so bitter, works so sweetly

Sometimes I feel like the petals of a

rose.

Sometimes I just see the thorns.

but it will not change the

ultimate truth.

All parts of it make me whole.

Loving is hard.

It's easier to not love.

but for some people hating someone means the

death of them.

They would rather watch their souls bleed.

than to tear apart somebody
They would sew it for them.
while they are torn themselves.

Sometimes I feel like I am water.

so tranquil,

so versatile

Sometimes I feel like I am on fire.

so anguish, so full of power

when both of them collide.

No war ever happens, only the death of one.

No one wins; no one loses.

— a war where no one wins

They say I am beautiful.
Is it my eyes or what they see?

Is it my mouth or what it says?

Is it my skin or what it touches?

Is it the outer self or the internal me?

– beauty

god picks you up from the rubble

which people thought was ntohing but ashes

and then he makes you rise from the ashes

and you turn into fire,

use this fire to keep others warm,
make them feel loved when their bones are
cold.

thank you for loving me when i hated myself

thank you for understadning me

when i couldnt even understand myself

thank you for making me laugh

when it seemed alien to me

thank you for making me stay when i wanted to leave.

- to the ones who were there

You are not lost, my dear; you just haven't
found who you are.

Living is merely living if each one of your veins is
not runnning with plasma and passion.

For them, oxygen cylinders were taken out, and
I just asked for a pen and paper.

What are you up to these days?

Nothing much, just writing and visiting
expensive cafes,

tasting the poetry like how I want my coffee to
be

not too bitter or too sweet.

If the whole universe is fighting against your
happiness, you have to fight the whole universe
for your happiness.

It felt like I was born with the curse of unhappiness. Later, I realized I had cursed myself; I had cast the spells; only I could undo it, so I did. And I broke free from the curse that stopped me from living.

Coffee, art, and poetry keep me going. I do stop sometimes; it's those days when my coffee turns cold, my palette gets broken, and my pages are torn.

I gave up on the idea of living. Mom told me to live for her, and that's when I knew that she had been living for me too.

Nothing in this world is immortal except for the art that people create.

The future seemed like a tragic movie; I forgot to
live through the present, like how a caterpillar
waits for it to turn into a butterfly. That's when I
knew that the longer I waited for tomorrow, the
less I lived today.

In this silence, I stumble upon certain noises.

Loud enough to make me lose my mind.

Loud enough, but not enough for you to hear
Why am I deaf to the world, except for this?

Why is the world hearing all this except for this?

"When the spirits are high and the sun is shining on my face , I just feel a sense of warmth hugging me, not burning me with the sun's malice to ashes"

My soul is crushing, just like the autumn leaves

Someone steps on it and leaves an ugly mark.

Leaves are falling, just like I fell into a shallow
void.

My heart sinks into it, yet I feel like it's floating
on top.

The autumn breeze is singing a song of
melancholy.

The ones who aren't deaf to its sound can feel it
coming close slowly.

Everything is dying yet so beautiful.

Maybe it's not always about the tragedy, but the
perception.

The leaves will grow back when it's time.

Let the branches lament over 'em as they shed off.

The emptiness is a must to feel the crowdedness.

The one who leaves has a heavy heart.
The one they leave has an empty heart.
Every soul shall taste death, they say.
Let me stay in my agony until it's May.

Melancholy has my heart.

It never left my soul.

Engraved in each one of my bones

Like a permanent tattoo

It's kind of cliche how it loves me to death.
It might be the death of me; it might take away my
breath.

like a forbidden home, like a broken dome
like a nightmare that turned out to be true.

Like my happiness is at curfew.

Melancholy has my heart.

It never left my soul.

It stayed until there was nothing left.

It left me with quite a debt.

A feeling that can't be given birth to in words

An author who fell in love with its verse

The songs that reminds us

How can I let go? How can I let it not show?

A feeling that felt like a warm hug
A barista who fell in love with its coffee cup
The flavours that remind us

How can I not cry? Who would even let them

dry?

A feeling that felt like home
A rose that fell in love with its thorns
The smell that reminds us

How can I not know?

How can I kill this hope?
A feeling that felt like a funeral
A corpse that fell in love with its tomb
The grief that reminds us
How can I forget it all?
How can I break the wall?

The faucet of love kept flowing.

There is enough water to satisfy the thirst of
millions.

It just knew to give and give.

They mostly called this faucet too naive.

The days when the sun shone, shimmering

This faucet held a helpless hand.

It just knew to give and give.

They mostly called this faucet too naive.

It's a cold flow, more like a relief valve.

This faucet is the best at its job.

It just knew to give and give.

They mostly called this faucet too naive.

One day, this faucet freezes as it gets frosty outside.

People turn to the warm faucets to help their pride.

It just knew to give and give.

This faucet kept on flowing even when there was
nothing to come out of it.

This faucet kept on flowing just to let a
drop out of it.

piano keys, major and minor

Life plays one at a time.

A sweet melody heals my wounded parts.

A bitter melody breaks my heart.

piano keys, major and minor

Life plays both sometimes.

intertwined melody confuses my soul.

Whether it's willing to let the music flow
Whether it's willing to let the music go

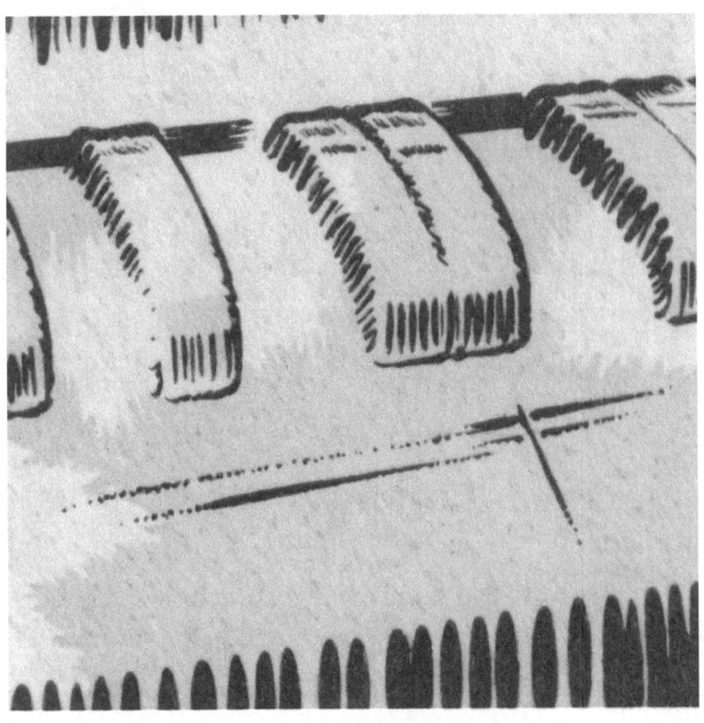

Chelsea boots:

I no longer wear shoes with laces.

I no longer want to wait for someone to tie them.

I prefer Chelsea boots.

They save me from misery or from turning numb.

Last time, I stepped on mine while I tried to tie
them.

I couldn't reach them, so I tried to hide them.

Nobody noticed, but I was crawling the whole time.

It seemed like I was walking, but it was a mirage I
had to mime.

For how long can you wait for someone to tie it for
you?

Would you ever stop wearing these shoes, or would
you go for something new?

Would you keep on crawling through your life just
for the sake of those shoes?

Or would you choose something that would help
you walk again like you used to?

Am I sad, or is sadness me?

I asked myself with an uplifted eyebrow.

Like an empty vessel waiting to be filled.

Knowingly, there is a hole in it.

There is beauty in hope.

But beauty fades away too.

Like hope does at a point,

All there are left are scars and wounds.

Am I sad, or is sadness me?

I asked myself with an uplifted eyebrow.

like a cloud waiting to move.

Knowingly, there is air sinking into it.

Like a wind waiting to be blown

Knowingly, there is nothing to hold.

like a boat waiting to reach the shore.

Knowingly, it is drowning deep in the ocean.

Am I sad, or is sadness me??

I no longer feel the need to know.

It no longer bothers me, as I made it my home.

A home that my soul hates, but the only place I
have got to stay

Like a bird waiting for the crew

Unknowingly, they all left a long time ago.

Like a penguin waiting for its mate

Knowingly, it died last spring.

Like a piece of tissue paper that is wet and won't
last long.

Like a rusted lock that won't be of any use.
Like a key that has lost its charm
Like a watch that has no arm to put on.

Am I sad, or is sadness me??

I said I didn't want to know, yet I asked again.

What is wrong with me?

What is right with me?

Like a traffic light that only shows a red light.
Like a telephone that has no line
Like a candle that has no wick.

like a lighter that has no fuel left in it.

I'm scared to say it, yet I did again.

Am I sad, or is sadness me?

I am getting frustrated.

I am biting my teeth.

What is wrong with me?

What is right with me?

like an actor who does comedy

movies.

Like an Oscar, whom people treat as a prized
possession

like a joker, I smile and not really smile.

Like a joker, I laugh, but not really laugh.

My, oh my, I hope I don't say it again.

Am I sad, or is sadness me??

Are my fingers working on their own?
Is it a spell that I have cast on myself?

Like oxygen, I am breathing it.
like carbon dioxide, I am exhaling it.
Like water, I am drinking it.
Like clothes, I am wearing them.

Am I sad, or is sadness me?
I asked it again, you see.
It never leaves my mind, ever.
It has built a grave there, forever.

Like a mummy waiting to be awakened
like a cold waiting to be caught.
Like autumn leaves waiting to wither
Like spring flowers waiting to bloom.

Am I sad, or is sadness me?
I asked it yet again, you see?
Nothing can change my mind.
Nothing can break this rhyme.

Like an old book, the scent remains.
Like a broken vase, the cracks remain.
Like shredded cheese, it's in pieces.
Like ice cream, it's melting away.

Am I sad, or is sadness me?

Oh god, stop it.

I am done, you see.

I am tired of it all.

I want to get away from this

feeling.

Like a grave waiting to be dug.

Like an egg waiting to hatch.

Like a star waiting to fall
Like a person falling out of love

Am I sad, or is sadness me?

God, are you even hearing me?

I said that I was tired.

Can't you see I want to run away from here.

Like a glacier melting too soon
Like somebody staring at the moon
Like a little kid looking for its mom
Like comedy, looking out for rom

Am I sad, or is sadness me?

Ugh, nvm, I get it at least.

I won't mind it now, as I have lost my mind.

I won't try to find an answer to this stupid noun.

All I see is sadness in everything.

Everything I see is sad indeed

A flair of happiness, a pinch of humour
But a lot more sad and sad.

I guess I am sad, as it is a whole of me.

Nobody can tell what's going on in my mind.

I am a genius, but I feel like I am cursed.

Nobody will ever know the tsunamis inside my

heart.

A poem that can never be written down without piercing your heart a million times

Still, you will find only a word or two to fill the gap between you and your muse.

The poetry that I write will not reach your heart if you don't let it.

I promise it will leave it soon.

as soon as you let it.

I feel like an idiot.

when I assume people will understand my words.

They have never, and they will never

Nobody knows my language better than I do.

They interpret my words and turn them into their own.

They left me feeling like I stole them from them, and they were never something that I owned.

Pain is kind of unbearable, you see.
This pain is lingering in my body like a fish
swimming in an ocean.

Is there a way to get rid of it?

Is there a way to unlive this fish?

They call me selfish for saying this.
Am I really selfish for taking care of this fish for
an eternity?

I got nothing in return but this pain.

Am I selfish, or am I just too selfless to exist?

There are more fish in the sea.

They are right in a way.

There are many fish in the sea.

Just not enough houses for them to stay

I gave them all a home.

And yet I'm selfish?

I gave them a reason to hold on.
And I'm the one who is selfish?

I am finally 21.

Life is far from fun.

Metaphoricaly drowning in my miseries

I wish I could turn back time.

Back to when I was 9
Growing up is a pain with no remedy.

I don't know why, but I feel so lost.

Lost in my mind

They keep on telling me

I will be fine.

I hope it's not a lie.

I'm holding up a gun.

To my head every time

When I feel like I don't deserve to live

They say I am precious.
But why don't I feel the same?

Like everyone else, someone tell me

Nobody understands how it feels

Until they get stuck in this vicious web

Your body feels paralyzed.

You can't move a thing.

"Sometimes we feel separated from ourselves. We are part of our bodies but not connected to them. It's like your whole world is on fire, and you are the one who ignited it in the firstplace. You can't help it but detest yourself for it. You make an effort to flee from yourself, but you never seem to be able to get away from the fire you have started. You can't afford to leave yourself alone in the fire that you have ignited. It's quite ironic when the whole world adores you except for you. They say that you are at the summit, but all you see from the top is a volcano waiting to explode. *All you see are flaws in you, and all you see is darkness.*"

"Getting attached is good until you feel yourself running after something. You keep on running and running; you blame your shoes for being so stiff; you blame the weather for being so cold; you blame yourself for being so slow because you can't seem to catch it. Some turn back and alter their goals, while others keep on running until they see the dead end. That's when their legs start to shake, their limbs get frozen, their hearts pace faster, and their breaths deepen. Are you still running, or have you reached the end yet? Do you intend to shift your focus to something else?"

"*When you are in mental warfare, your thoughts act as ammunition that no nation could purchase.* These weapons not only kill you but also deform you enough for you to hate yourself even more. No doctor could help you save yourself when you are at war with yourself; no medicine would taste bitterer than your existence when you are at war with yourself. When you grow up in a place that seems like it's on fire, you don't know how coldness feels, yet paradoxically, your heart is so frigid and your feet are so chilly that you end up detesting yourself deeply.

You point fingers at everything, but it never makes things right. You sense everything too intensely and deeply enough for you to feel powerless"

When you hear the sound of bones breaking,
you indeed feel horrified, but when you feel
your soul breaking, you are traumatised.

Even these tsunamis were not enough to drown
my house of hope;

even these tsunamis were not enough to unthaw
my tightrope.

I find peace in my choas. Thats why I prefer dinlas over eros.

I streched my fractured spine to tie your shoes,
and you blamed me for the sound that came with
the hurt.

Don't waste time painting other people and then whining about how black and white you are.

maybe its about the perception and not the tragedy

When a child only knows the difference between white chocolate and milk chocolate, how is this child supposed to know the difference between hurting your toe or hurting your soul?

until they've had a taste of both.

The existence of a lunar crescent, albeit its incompleteness, is very beautiful.

Like you, even at times when you don't feel whole, you are complete.

That one house seems so familiar every time I walk into it. Every time I walk into it, someone locks the door from outside.

That someone is no one but me.
That house is nothing but my past memories.

I was an avid reader until I received your

letter. I forgot every language,

and I forgot how to read.

These migrating birds, these moving clouds, and this melting ice cream and skin turning to wrinkles give me a sigh of relief.

It tells me that nothing stays constant, nothing stays the same.

If you could meet anyone from your past, what would you say, and whom would you meet?

I would meet little me, and I wouldn't say anything but give her a tight hug until her heart stopped to weep.

I jumped into the fire to save you, and even though I was inflammable, you ran away as if my ashes were invisible.

My death is looming when I sting like a honeybee.

For the intent of explaining agony, I am like a hyperbole.

When a child trips and falls, he feels injured, sobs, and then gets back up and continues playing.

Why do adults perceive falling as an omen of failure when it's evidently just an inevitable part of life?

Why do we believe that adults are incapable of failing?

Who pulls this word from their dictionary?

I keep asking myself if I'm lost or if I was never found.

I nevertheless continue hearing a voice that whispers I'm both lost and found at the same.

we were like the letter I but we divereged like Y

Healing is painful, but not healing is
catastrophic.
Which suffering would you let to be your
demise?

i know how it feels to be nothing but something.

My condolences; I have strangled myself a
million more times and have seen myself die a
thousand times.

For what would your mouth twitch if all was said?

My dread is not horror films; rather, it is monsters that pose as human beings.

"Lets move to the moon?"

why not make earth
worth living on?

your soul is so pure

Like 24 carat gold

you dont even know

the power that you hold
wish i could let you know

I could only hear noises in the silence, and silence
in the noises.

pain makes us feel lost
like warmth in the frost

this paper town never felt like home i
want a paper town that i can call my
own.

They say that I have the aura of spring, but I really feel reminiscent of fall.

I find beauty in things that are dying and in things falling apart.

Why do I keep on fixing paper people when all
they do is crumble down?

An author is born when he
dies, an ideal instance of
reincarnation in disguise.

You were deaf to my melody, and I was deaf to
mine;

all I could hear was your music,
which you never played for me.

Why is it so hard to be happy?

when it takes nothing to be

sad.

This fish would kill me if I didn't do the
same.
Life is an epitomy of a
political game.

I polished your filthy high boots.
You took them off, complaining they were
loose. I mended them for you.
You said you no longer wear those shoes.

There was a time.

when I was trying to catch falling stars above my rooftop

thinking I was so smart.

But who knew that the real stars were on the ground?

like one is you.

There was a time.

When I doubted myself, I thought that I wasn't enough.

I am sure you have been through it too.

So I wrote this poem for you.

When it gets hard, don't forget.

You are a star.

You always shine and shine and shine.

You are like a rainbow in someone's dark sky.

I know we all need someone sometimes.

If you don't have someone, let me hear your inner voice.

I will be your friend. I will listen to your pain.

When life falls apart, don't forget.

You are a star.

You light up so many lives.

You shine the brightest in the sky.

Like a dandelion, the little breeze scatters

me; I am split, and all over

the place,

I am as fragile as a vintage vase.

Yesterday, I was looking through your pictures.
The one smile that makes my heart warm

If I had a chance, I would have said hold on.

But now you are already gone.
I still remember the blue jacket that you used to
make me wear.

I would make angry faces as you combed down my
hair.

I regret the times we fought like bears.

I really do, and I miss you.

But I know that you know

You are always on my mind, and I can't let you go.

As I sleep and breathe in, I think of you.

And I just want to let you know.

I love you.

But you know that I know.

You watch everything that I do.

You know me better than anyone out here. No
one can replace you; no one can fill your space.

I miss you, and I wish you were here.

- for a friend who lost her mom

The flight attendants advise passengers to take care of themselves before trying to aid others when the oxygen level drops.

Every time I hear that, it gets to me hard.

Someone will always put others' needs ahead of their own.

People who allow it to happen will always exist.

There will always be some who are desperate to rescue themselves.

and some people are going to run out of oxygen.

When life throws lemons at you,

some say make lemonade,

some say throw them in your eyes,

some say make lemon cake,

and some say sell them at a higher price.

When life throws lemons at you,

I say do nothing.

You don't have to make lemonade or bake a cake;
you just have to let the lemons run out until you
can walk away from there.

Would you press a button to take your own life right then and there?

If not, i feel happy for you.

If yes, you have to fight until you refuse to hit that button.

That button is just your subconscious asking you to go.

My love, please turn it off, turn it off, and turn it down.

You have to stay here.

Nothing is eternal.

Why, in your perspective, would this

pain?It's not at all that passionate.

its not here to stay.

some faces seem so bright, like a flashlight.

Their light is enough to conceal the sinister
thoughts in their minds.

When you turn off this light, you see that they have
been fighting for their lives.

They seemed so bright; who would have thought
they were dying from inside?

When I close my eyes, I see nothing. When I
open my eyes, I see nothing.

I am not blind, but a fool. I am dwelling in a
never ending loop.

I heard songs that nobody ever sang. I
heard music that nobody ever played.
Oh my, am I dreaming of this melody?
Then it must be gatekept.

Words are lethal drugs;

no one forewarns you about them.

thoughts add fuel to the fire of your burning
desire.

I might catch a cold instead and let out phelgm.

Just as I spit it out, I spit my words on paper.

to know I am cold, I am sick, and I am a little
frailer.

Like a fever dream, I see this life
as a song of different genres,
a song that I don't like,
but I keep hearing it again and again.
I still don't know a single lyric; I am
quite mundane.
How will I sing this song when it's time?
How will I know when to start a single line?
How foolish of me to just hear and not
understand.
Maybe then this song would have taken over my
favourite band.

I am like parallel lines, so close yet so far.

So separated from myself, like peace is with

war.

To save the legacy of poets, I chose to turn into
one.

Who knew that poetry was my language and the
only language I actually knew?

Poetry, like healing, is a
process. Though writing it
hurts, it also comforts.

My pupil enlarges as if I were in love.
nevertheless I'm too maniac, and I have little
idea how to love.

Isn't it funny how dreams are made?

When your reality starts to fade, you start
cursing your fate.

Then you start changing your fate.

Then you start chasing your dreams.

You both meet when you are standing on the

cliff, One step away from falling deep into it.

People want to be millionaires. There's nothing
wrong with it.

but I want to own a coffee shop near a place in
Italy.

For every muse, I would make art. how beautiful
life would be, I wish I can live this dream,

I wish I can live this dream.

I smile a lot more often than I used to.

I smile about the fact that I thought this pain would never leave.

But it left too.

Be kind to your mind, is what they say.
I say, be kind to every single bone of
yours. Every part of you deserves love.
Your soul deserves the biggest hug.

its not a full stop, but a semicolon.

letter to the reader:

Hey there beautiful human beings! I will get straight to the point. Don't let anyone ever tell you that something is too good for you. Nothing is too good for you. I was told in 4th grade that I wouldn't be able to do well in English literature. I felt shattered and unworthy of anything, but I didn't give up. and here I am, writing my own book. wrote my own story. I am not a bestselling author yet, but I am an author. Nobody can tell you what you can or cannot do; it all depends on you. Hear me out: The day you stop caring if you are going to fail is the day you are getting there. From one soul to another, you are worthy of everything, and your dreams are going to come true one day. If you feel lost and found at the same time, just like me, don't worry; I get you, and I know you get me too.

All the best for everything!

Love, shaista samreen

a message to the men out there,

I hope that you are doing okay; even if you are not, it is totally okay. You are a human being, and you have the right to feel all the emotions just like the rest of us. You can laugh out loud on your happy days and cry your heart out when the days are tough. People say that men shouldn't cry, and if they do, they aren't men, but I

think, and I am telling you, not crying does not make you a man, but being vulnerable with your emotions and speaking your heart out makes you a man;

it makes you a human after all. Your feelings are important, and if someone tells you the opposite, they are just not a human being in the first place. The money you earn does not define you, but how you treat yourself and others around you defines you in a deeper sense.

So if you think that you are not worthy just because you are not a millionaire yet, you are worth more than millions of dollars. Just because your soul is so beautiful, it is not quantifiable. Don't let this cruel society tell you who you are and who you can be; you decide your destiny and work for it. You do everything that makes you happy in the right sense, and you keep on being you, little gentleman.

a message to the ladies out there,

How are you? How has it been going? I'm a complete stranger asking this, but I won't be able to hear your answer. I'm kind of sad for it, but you are there for yourself. I just wanted to let you know that you are so darn beautiful, not only from the outside but from the inside as well. You might be wondering, How does she know this? I just know. Your body, your hair, your thoughts, and your scars-everything is so beautiful about you. You deserve the world, honey. You deserve everything. Never let the world tell you otherwise. You are a queen, and your brain is your royalty. much love for you.

a message for someone who is struggling to stay,

Hi there, If you are struggling with your mental health and it's getting hard to stay here, I just wanted to let you know that unaliving yourself is like getting in a room with a bomb filled with all the people that you love. You not only unalive yourself but everyone who loves you. I know that when we are in a state of mind where everything is just too dark and pointless, the only way out we find is this. I don't know if this will change your mind or not, but I want to give you some reasons to stay, and while you checklist them, I hope your mind changes one by one.

Just from a random stranger, please don't leave. If I could, I would beg down on my knees.

you can watch the sunrise everyday, maybe as sun rises so does hope in you, you can watch the sunset evryday, maybe when sun sets so does your withering thoughts, you can see the stars my dear friend, maybe how they seem to twinkle will ignite a spark in you, you can talk to yoir friends, maybe their jokes will make it better for you, you can paint the starrynight maybe it will light up your darkest nights, you can go to the beach, maybe the sand castle will make you happy, you can go to the mountain top, maybe it will help you see soemhting that isnt visible, you can write down your thoughts, maybe you will become a bestselling author, you can talk to old people, maybe they will tell you things that nobody would ever, you can do a lot more, maybe it will make you stay here forevermore. i always say that maybe its about the perception and not the tragedy.

If you decide to go right now, you might miss out on the life that could have been so beautiful-a life that you always desired.

We give so many chances to people; we give so many chances to things; why not give yourself more chances until you feel like living again?

I love you; I really mean it. I am really proud of you.

National Suicide Prevention Helpline1800-121-3667

The Helpline provides 24/7, free and confidential support for people in distress,

prevention and crisis resources for you or your loved ones.